Angels *at the* Bedside

SPIRITUAL STORIES FROM AN
INTUITIVE HOSPICE NURSE

Lynda Noll

BALBOA.PRESS
A DIVISION OF HAY HOUSE

Copyright © 2021 Lynda Noll.

All rights reserved. No part of this book may be used or reproduced by any means, graphic, electronic, or mechanical, including photocopying, recording, taping or by any information storage retrieval system without the written permission of the author except in the case of brief quotations embodied in critical articles and reviews.

Balboa Press books may be ordered through booksellers or by contacting:

Balboa Press
A Division of Hay House
1663 Liberty Drive
Bloomington, IN 47403
www.balboapress.com
844-682-1282

Because of the dynamic nature of the Internet, any web addresses or links contained in this book may have changed since publication and may no longer be valid. The views expressed in this work are solely those of the author and do not necessarily reflect the views of the publisher, and the publisher hereby disclaims any responsibility for them.

The author of this book does not dispense medical advice or prescribe the use of any technique as a form of treatment for physical, emotional, or medical problems without the advice of a physician, either directly or indirectly. The intent of the author is only to offer information of a general nature to help you in your quest for emotional and spiritual well-being. In the event you use any of the information in this book for yourself, which is your constitutional right, the author and the publisher assume no responsibility for your actions.

Any people depicted in stock imagery provided by Getty Images are models, and such images are being used for illustrative purposes only. Certain stock imagery © Getty Images.

Content editing by Parthenia Hicks.
Cover design by Jennifer Stimson.
Author cover photo courtesy of Twyla Hall.

https://lyndanoll.com

Print information available on the last page.

ISBN: 978-1-9822-7753-6 (sc)
ISBN: 978-1-9822-7755-0 (hc)
ISBN: 978-1-9822-7754-3 (e)

Library of Congress Control Number: 2021923287

Balboa Press rev. date: 11/17/2021

Gratitude

"Dad" who recognized my talent for writing as a child and encouraged me to develop this gift. Through his own death while on hospice, I discovered not only my spiritual calling as a hospice nurse but also the subject of my writing that I hope honors him and helps many others. I am grateful he is always available to me in spirit.

Paul, my husband, who encouraged me to get busy and get this book done. His words were, "You've always wanted to write this book, and now it's time to get it done." His love and support have always been a blessing through our marriage and raising a family, and throughout my nursing career.

Lindy, my daughter, who followed me into healthcare as a social worker. I am grateful she has chosen me as her mom and that she has chosen a career of service. We uniquely support each other in the empathetic work of caring for others. This book reaches out to her and all providers in offering the wisdom of strength and resilience through self-care.

Andrew, my son, who helped me with marketing and brought a fresh and creative perspective to my biography and website. I appreciate how you have blessed me with being your mom in this lifetime.

Parthenia, an awesome writing coach who, most of all, understands my spiritual perspective and vision for this book. Her initial and continuing commitment and encouraging words helped me realize the vision of my book was possible. She has helped me put this book together in a meaningful way, polishing it to an elegant sheen. I like to think she was sent to me as an answer to prayer. She was the one called to help me.

Buddy and Baxter, my dogs, who patiently kept me company and hogged part of my chair throughout this writing. They encouraged me to take breaks (for playtime, snuggles, treats, feeding, walks) and enabled me to return each time with a fresh perspective.

My guardian angels, who have always been with me through this lifetime. Gosh, the ups and downs must have been a challenge for you. I am so very grateful for your ongoing support.

My deceased patients and their families, whose relationships, however briefly on this earth, I appreciate and honor. As I wrote my book, I could sometimes feel their presence helping me remember significant details. I appreciate that you have helped me grow into a stronger spiritual connection with the Divine.

This book is dedicated to my patients, who briefly graced my life with their stories, their sadness, their joys, their encounters with their own angels, and their courage to face the mystery of leaving this plane.

All of these stories are true. However, the names of the dying and their family members are purely fictitious and have been changed for privacy considerations.

Contents

Gratitude v
Dedication ix
Introduction: The Book I Was Called to Write
and Perhaps You Were Called to Read xv

Chapter 1:   My Journey to Hospice 1
       Losing My Dad 1
       Visits from the Divine: An Intuitive Perspective ...5
       Near Car Accident 6
       Lost Eyeglasses 7
       The Grand Prize 8
       Damselflies and Dragonflies 10
       A Red Koi Fish on New Year's Day 11
       Ducks: An Unusual Answer to Prayer 11

Chapter 2:   What Is Hospice? 13
       Misconceptions 13
       The Hospice Nurse and Team 15
       The Labor of Death: What It Looks Like 16
       Signs of Progressive Decline 18

Chapter 3:   Saying Goodbye 20
   Mark and Josefina: Comforting
   Words from a Spouse with Dementia 21
   Joe and Lisa: Daddy's Girl Says Goodbye 23

Chapter 4:   How the Dying Choose
   When They Pass 26
   Victor and Rhonda: Choosing the
   Time of Death to Make It Easier on
   Your Spouse 27
   Carlos and Lucia: A Nurse's Intuitive Knowing ... 29

Chapter 5:   Comforting Visions of Spirits 32
   Sarah: Visions of Deceased Family Members 33
   Carol: Visions of Jesus 34

Chapter 6:   Opening to Spirit Talk 36
   Richard: Channeling Words to a Daughter 37
   Ruth: Intuitive Reception of the Perfect Words ... 39
   Self-Care for Caregivers 41

Chapter 7:   Angels as Guides 43
   Katharina: Angels Arrive at
   the Time of Death 44
   Ethel: Intuiting Angels at the Bedside 46
   John: A Procession of Angels in Human Form ... 48

Chapter 8:   Healing Grief with Love 50
  Christina and David: Healing
  through Photos and Deep Listening 51
  Rosa: A Comfortable Death
  Experience Heals the Family............................53
  Andres and Wanda: Changing the
  Grief Perspective 56
  Pablo and Judy: Pablo Heals Judy and
  His Caregivers 58

Chapter 9:   Sharing Love through Nutrition..............60
  Betty and Cindy: Feeding an
  Unconscious Mom 61
  Lois and Anne: The Struggle with a
  Mom Who Refuses to Eat.................................63
  June and Beth: Hydration Isn't a Priority 64

Chapter 10: How Forgiveness Heals the Dying
  and the Living 67
  Mabel: Forgiveness Heals an
  Unresponsive Mom and Her Daughters 68
  Doris: Daughters Forgive Each Other
  to Help Mom Pass 69

Chapter 11: Comfort through Religion, Music,
 Medicine, and Intuition...........................71
 Jack: Finding Comfort through the
 Music of His Church..72
 Annie: The Power of Music to Reach
 Dementia Patients 74
 Leticia: Offering Comfort without Medicine....75
 Nonverbal Signs of Pain: Ways to
 Determine if a Person May Be in Pain..............78

Chapter 12: Prayer to Help the Dying.......................79
 Virginia: Praying for Healing at the Bedside.... 80
 Aileen: "Your Prayers Are Answered!"..............82
 Manuel: Praying for a Way to Communicate 84
 Praying for the Dying through Poetry..............85
 I Will Pray for You 87

Final Thoughts 89
About the Author..91

Introduction

THE BOOK I WAS CALLED TO WRITE AND PERHAPS YOU WERE CALLED TO READ

*D*eath and dying aren't subjects most people want to talk about. Many would rather reveal their most intimate secrets than spend five minutes thinking about the dying process—theirs, or that of someone they're close to. While death and hospice are both difficult subjects, this is the world I have lived in and come to embrace, both professionally and personally.

Angels at the Bedside is written from my heartfelt journey as a hospice nurse. Through my work with the dying, I have found a meaningful life, a calling. This book is a collection of end-of-life stories based on my experience caring for hundreds of people. I share these true stories with you in hopes of bringing an awareness of the overwhelming potential each of us has to bring love and healing into the relationships we have with our departing loved ones.

As a child, I understood that intuition was a magical—perhaps even mystical—gift. Over the years, I have learned to tune into this gift and trust it. You will see how following my intuition has helped me, and others, through difficult times as I integrated this into my hospice work. Working as a hospice nurse has been not only a journey of heart opening but one of embracing the spirit that I believe is always with us, especially at the bedside during our end-of-life transition. Through my perspective, I hope you will gain insight into new ways of being present at the bedside of your loved one. My greatest hope is that while learning to become more present at the bedside of your loved one, you will also learn ways to bring healing to your loved one—and therefore to yourself. It's absolutely never too late.

In our culture, dying is intimately tied to religion. Unfortunately, religion sometimes has a way of separating people through the belief that only "my religion" is right. This book is written for any person of any religious belief. Although I was raised Christian, I consider myself a spiritual person and supportive of all beliefs. We are all on our own journeys, free to choose a religious path that helps us understand the meaning of our life. Part of life is the end of life—death. My work has brought me closer to the belief that there may be an afterlife, perhaps a specific place, where people move on to after death. I know there is a living essence, which I call spirit, that exists around us everywhere, supporting us in our daily lives and in the hard times, including dying.

I have seen and experienced the profound grief that comes with dying. It is tough to understand and witness our dying loved ones in physical decline, confused, hallucinating, nauseous, eating poorly, in pain, or withdrawing socially. In the dying process, we often lose the people as we know them, and we grieve every step of the way. If we focus exclusively on fearful appearances, however, we miss the big picture and the opportunity to connect with our loved ones as they move through one of the most profound moments of their existence.

Through the end-of-life decline, there is often fighting between family members and grief expressed as anger. My hope is that by walking through these stories with me, you will not only feel the love within your family relationships but also know they can be strengthened, even at the end of life. When our family connections are braced by love, we are better prepared for the death of our loved ones. At this time, we need each other more than ever. When we die, love doesn't end—it remains, and it is my belief that those who have died before us stay with us.

My additional hope is that from hearing these stories,

you will embrace the opportunity to see the end-of-life experience—dying—as a chance to participate in a comforting, uplifting passage from this plane to the next, no matter your spiritual or religious belief system. I also hope you will come to appreciate the love that caregivers—whether family members or hospice nurses—bring to the dying experience, offering empathetic and even empathic healing to our loved ones.

Angels at the Bedside begins with a story about my personal journey to hospice through the death of my dad. The next chapter defines and describes hospice, which is the setting for the stories in this book. Subsequent chapters are organized around spiritual themes: saying goodbye; how and why the dying choose the time they want to pass; how visions of spirits are comforting; spirit talk; presence and empathetic listening; angels as guides during the dying process; healing relationships through grief with love; sharing love through understanding end-of-life nutritional changes; how forgiveness heals the dying and the living; comfort through religion, music, medicine and intuition; and offering prayer to help the dying pass more easily and comfortably. I also offer insight about how to recognize decline in a dying loved one as well as how to recognize nonverbal signs of pain. In addition, I emphasize self-care for caregivers—friends and family who are tending to a dying loved one. In this way, I hope to gently guide you through and beyond the fear that comes with the dying experience.

For those of you who work in the hospice industry—nurses, nursing aids, social workers, and chaplains—I hope these stories of unconditional love feed your soul. May the love contained within them bring healing to the difficult, challenging, and important work you offer to your patients.

Chapter 1
MY JOURNEY TO HOSPICE

Losing My Dad

My dad was in hospice care, and I was consumed with the thought that he was going to die. I simply wasn't ready. I remembered playing house with my imaginary friend as a four-year-old child, moving boxes that represented furniture into the shadows of the house. As we played, we watched the shadows begin to disappear with the sun's movement. Dad was like that shadow now, seeming to fade away. He was at home, too weak to move in the bed, confused, and certainly not the dad I remembered.

In his younger days in the military, Dad could do a push-up with one finger on one hand while his other hand was behind his back. I had always relied on his advice when making sense of emotional things. There was the time I was driving an old Buick purchased just days before. At a stoplight, we were rear-ended by a drunk driver. Dad reached over and held me in my seat, saying, "It's going to be okay, Lynda." My heart was beating so fast, yet I felt comfort not only in the tone of his voice but also in his mere presence. He would help me get through this.

I had been a nurse for many years working in a hospital. My patients were critically ill and needed lifesaving treatments. They were on ventilators that breathed for them, with medications going into their veins through tubes. Their heartbeats were monitored on screens. During family visits, limited to thirty minutes a few times a day, I would generally step out with the thought of giving them their privacy. Now, here I was witnessing the end-of-life decline in my dad. This time it wasn't a patient. It was my dad, and it was personal.

Mary, a stocky, middle-aged nurse five feet tall with short brown hair pulled up into a bun, had just finished checking Dad's vitals. I met her in the kitchen as she was washing her hands. I tried to hold back tears as I nervously blurted out, "I think he needs more pain medication, and maybe he's depressed."

Mary firmly and calmly replied, "Sometimes we need to step out of the role of nurse and just be the daughter." Tears came rolling down my face. I had been given permission to cry. Mary embraced me in a firm hug for what seemed like a full minute. Neither of us said anything. In that moment, as I was grieving for my dad's inevitable passing, I knew she understood me. She was not only a nurse but a compassionate soul. Her expression of love was just what I needed.

Mary's compassionate response to my grief deepened my own understanding of love and the meaning of loss in our family. In that moment as she warmly embraced me, I decided this was the kind of nurse I wanted to be. I was discovering my spiritual calling. I wanted to help the dying and their families in hospice to heal through love. I had been a nurse most of my adult life, but it wasn't until that moment fifteen years ago that I made the decision to become a hospice nurse.

As a child, I had the opportunity to experience two very different religions. Both my parents wanted me to learn the faith in which they strongly believed. This meant going from early Catholic mass to the Mormon church service in the same morning. Sometimes after mass, Mom would be waiting in the station wagon with the car running, eager to rush us off to her own church. To a degree, my parents' separate religious beliefs challenged the wholeness and love of our family being. Eventually, my mom and dad realized the growing rift over religion in their marriage and its potential to break up our family.

We stopped going to church so much and sporadically attended each church as Mom or Dad offered. We were given the opportunity to choose which church we wanted to attend and encouraged to think about which religion we would like to continue in our adult lives. By respecting the validity of their individual religions, my parents had risen to the highest level of the teachings of their religions. The love taught by all faiths and a loving marriage was more important than their particular religions.

From this upbringing, I felt it was my birthright to question religion. What I eventually came to realize is that people choose a particular religion as their path to discover spiritualty or universal love. Universal love is the understanding that we are all connected through the spirit of love to each other and all that is, regardless of religion.

As a nurse and creative spirit, I truly love my patients and strive to offer them the best of me. I am grateful for the love that I have been privileged to share with the dying and their families. Dying is as intimate and sacred as being born. The baby coming into this life and the dying person moving into the next life are both making sacred transitions. Being allowed into the privacy of the homes and hearts of those nearing death as the family shares its history of love through a lifetime together is an honor. I admit that I'm one of those hospice nurses who has continued to grieve many deaths because I allowed myself to fully invest my love in the care of patients who became another family to me. By writing this book, I am in a way processing my own grief and balancing the sadness by recalling memorable relationships and spiritual connections.

Hospice nurses are trained to address the spiritual, social, emotional, psychological, and physical needs of the dying patient and family. There is a paucity of research to define or explain what spirituality is. This book is an experiential example of spirituality in nursing. It is a way to explain a difficult concept to grasp in a science-based community. Here are just a few incidents that illustrate ways I've personally experienced spirit, or "divinely unexplainable support." I believe they will offer insight into how my spirituality and intuition naturally overflow into my work as a hospice nurse.

Visits from the Divine: An Intuitive Perspective

While I was growing up, I remember my mom and dad often saying, "Get your head out of the clouds!" Through daydreaming, I created my own world. As I grew older, I simply knew things, felt things, or heard things that I couldn't explain. At an early age, I became fascinated with life after death and the ability of others to be intuitive and develop mediumship. Through reading many books, and with practice, I was able to recognize and develop my own abilities to communicate with spirit.

We all have this gift, and like any gift, it is something we have to believe in and nurture if we want to experience it fully. Naturally, I would be drawn toward a healing profession while also embracing the spirit to assist me in caring for people in my own creative way. Occurrences that might be dismissed as coincidence to others are often more meaningful to me; I consider some of them as divine guidance. I vibrate in my heart and soul by paying attention to unusual signs. I believe that our loved ones who have passed are still looking after us. Our guardian angels and other special angels are available to support us as well. At times, I can feel my father's presence when I take daily walks in the park or neighborhood. He is present with me when I go through something difficult and pray actively for support.

Near Car Accident

I was driving my car home from a Spanish class that I was taking at a local community college, feeling sad, and thinking of my dad's recent passing. My car was a little Volkswagen, and I was in the left lane heading west. I came to an intersection where the light was red, and when I stopped, I heard a voice scream, "Watch out!" I was a little perplexed because there was no one else in the car with me, the windows were up, and the radio was off. Then I heard the shout—"Watch out!"—again.

I looked up at the ceiling of the car and said, "Watch out for what?"

I heard someone say, "She can hear you; you don't need to yell." This made me chuckle. The light in the opposite direction where cars were traveling east had turned green while my westbound car was still stopped on red. Two cars coming east in adjacent lanes suddenly accelerated and raced each other, coming toward me. One veered out of his lane, nearly hitting me, but at the last second he recovered and continued past me through the light. I suddenly understood the message. I was so grateful to be alive. Dad had taught me how to drive. He had been in a car accident with me. Now here he was in the afterlife, saving my life.

Lost Eyeglasses

My daughter was a flautist in sixth grade beginning band. Our family was on the way out the door for her concert, and I was the last one to get into the car with my son. My daughter said, "Momma, I lost my glasses."

Thinking that she would certainly need her glasses in order to read the music, I said, "Okay, let me go find them fast."

To which my daughter responded, "How are you going to do that?" Apparently, she had been looking for them for the last hour herself and had given up.

I ran inside, went up the stairs, and quickly made my way down the hallway to her room. I suddenly stopped in the doorway as if that was what I was directed to do. I looked up to the ceiling in her room. As I stood there alone, I asked, "Now, where are her glasses?" Instantly my instinct was to look down, where I saw the laundry basket full of clothes. I reached down and quickly removed several dirty shirts, a pair of shorts, some socks, and undies. Underneath her clothes were the glasses. I grabbed them and ran back down the hall, down the stairs, and back out to the car.

My daughter looked at me amazed and said, "How did you find them so fast?"

I responded, "I just asked and then 'knew' they were in the laundry basket."

She responded, "But who did you ask, and how did you know where to look?"

The Grand Prize

I was in between hospice jobs and decided to attend a three-day quilting retreat. I had no idea who might be there, but my attitude was that I would go alone and make new friends. This would be a much-needed way for me to relax and enjoy some time off. Because I had been so busy working, I had lost touch with many of my quilting friends. At the retreat, we socialize, eat, and sleep at the facility. It's a fun thing to do—as the quilts assemble, we all get to admire everyone's creative work. As it turns out, I ran into an old quilting friend who had worked with me at a former hospice. We had a lot in common, so my prayer to enjoy the retreat was partly answered by this renewal of an old friendship—although by the time I left, I had nineteen new friends!

At the retreat, we played silly games with prizes that were usually sewing related. Before one game, we were shown the prize of an overflowing basket of threads, sewing notions, embroidery floss, fabric rolls, knitting supplies, yarn, needles, and patterns. As I admired the basket, I heard my deceased dad ask, "Lynda, would you like to win the grand prize?" *Wow*, I thought, *that was loud and clear.* Then I thought, *Well, sure ... that would be great.*

Twenty of us sat down at a long series of tables to play a dice game. As the dice were rolled, we passed the fabric squares to the left or right, depending on the number showing on the rolled dice. With each pass, someone dropped out because they hadn't received any squares. Nineteen people dropped out of the game before I became the final winner, with one hundred fabric squares. I actually felt a little guilty for having won because I knew I'd had an unlikely accomplice. Nevertheless, I was grateful knowing my dad was with me not just in traumatic events but even in fun and peaceful moments.

Damselflies and Dragonflies

Spirit communicates with me through nature. Once, on an afternoon walk in the park, I offered my finger to a damselfly. She took me up on the offer and gracefully landed there, staying for about twenty minutes. I was mesmerized by the detail of her big eyes looking curiously at me. I felt this visit was a way for Spirit to let me know She was present. I'd experienced a damselfly landing on me two other times, and each time it had felt divinely directed.

Once, I was riding in the passenger seat of the car with the window open, traveling about forty miles per hour. A delicate dragonfly overcame the force of the wind, flew through the window, and landed on my hand. I watched it as we traveled, and fifteen minutes later, it flew as easily away, out the window. I have since taken numerous pictures of dragonflies, who in some cultures are considered mystically to be deceased spirits. At any rate, these creatures seem drawn to me, easily resting on or near me. My husband jokes that this doesn't happen for him.

A Red Koi Fish on New Year's Day

I was at a recreational lake park on January 1, New Year's Day. I had been praying for a better year with less stress and more joy. I walked to the water's edge and looked down to see a beautiful bright red koi fish, unusual in this area, swim up to me and linger just beyond where I was standing. I felt this was a sign from the Divine. My prayer would be answered. That was the first and the last time I would ever see a koi in this lake.

Ducks: An Unusual Answer to Prayer

My daughter decided she wanted to find and purchase her first home. She no longer wanted to rent an apartment and was determined to move. I had prayed fervently that we would find the perfect home for her. We had already been looking but hadn't found just the right one.

It was a crisp October morning as I walked through the neighborhood, thinking how hopeful I was for her to find a home where she would be happy. The skies were a light gray with a misty, moist air. I came to a corner on the sidewalk and saw three ducks just across the quiet two-lane residential street. Two were a bright white with orange beaks and feet; one was smaller, a mottled white and brown. I stood still as the quacking ducks eyed me across the road and waddled toward me. I got the impression that they were coming specifically to see me. They seemed to be happy and were quacking away. I was worried for their safety, so I guided them back across the road where there was a drainage pond. After we crossed, I walked down the hill to the pond's edge and stood there, hoping they would go in the water, but instead they siphoned through the grass near my feet and kept quacking. The color of their bright orange beaks was in contrast to my blue tennis shoelaces. I started walking slowly around the pond with the ducks waddling just behind me. Intermittently, I would stop to see if they would get in the water. My hope was that they would become distracted and wade into the water so I could continue my walk. After I had gotten three-quarters around the pond, they found the grass really interesting and got lost in their feeding. I moved away slowly and then hurried away from the pond and back up to the sidewalk.

    I had never before seen these ducks at this drainage area on any of my daily walks. I have also not seen them since. They certainly caught my attention because ducks from my childhood are still memorable in my heart. I considered that maybe Dad was sending me the message that he would help us find that perfect home. Later that morning, we went to the realtor's house so she could drive us around to look at property. I could feel Dad's presence with us. As it turned out, we would find just the right home by day's end.

Chapter 2
WHAT IS HOSPICE?

Misconceptions

There are many misconceptions about hospice. The very word *hospice* is associated with fear of death. Any words of explanation that follow it are often not even heard by patients or their loved ones. The listener simply blocks the remaining conversation. Many people are not ready to hear, think about, or discuss death. Let's clear up some of the misconceptions that exist around hospice.

Hospice is a philosophy of care rather than a place. Quality of life is the priority, and comfort is paramount. This is in contrast to quantity of life and strategies to prolong life regardless of the pain and suffering the person may be in. Hospice is delivered anywhere a person calls home, including assisted living facilities and nursing homes. It is also provided in freestanding hospice facilities and hospitals. Most people, when asked, would prefer to die at home, surrounded by familiar surroundings and the comfort of those they love. Sadly, death often happens in the cold environment of the hospital with life-prolonging machines and medications, and without family who may not or cannot be present.

One misconception about hospice is that the person in hospice is imminently dying. This is not always true. To be admitted to hospice means that the dying and their families understand an estimated life expectancy (remaining lifetime) of six months or less. Life expectancy is based on the physician's experience and knowledge of the disease process. As long as a dying person continues to decline, they will remain on hospice—sometimes for years. And people can and do get better and improve. When this happens, they will be discharged back to routine care. Should the person worsen again, hospice could be reconsidered.

Hospice is about supporting the person through the expected decline that comes through the disease. Specifically, it is about providing comfort. Another erroneous belief is that when a dying person receives a stronger medication, such as morphine, hospice is causing the loved one to die. Hospice does not give medications to push people to their deaths. Instead, these medications are offered in order to help the person to be comfortable—to help them breathe more slowly and easily so when the time comes for them to pass, they are able to let go without struggling. A normal breathing rate is eight to twelve breaths a minute, but a dying person's breathing rate can sometimes be as high as fifty or even sixty times a minute. By giving morphine, the patient has a more comfortable death, and the family also has a better dying experience.

Hospice does not separate the dying person from the family; in fact, it treats them as one. The closest relationships I formed with my dying patients were developed after spending considerable time getting to know them and their families. Sadly, many people come to hospice within the last few days or weeks of their lives, so this special bond between the hospice team is not formed.

The Hospice Nurse and Team

What is a hospice team? The hospice team consists of a medical doctor, a nurse, an aid (who helps with bathing, dressing, and grooming), a nondenominational chaplain, and a social worker. They work together in the care of the dying and the family. The nurse makes weekly visits at first and increases visits as time comes closer to the end. Hospice also includes twenty-four-hour availability of a nurse through an on-call system. Essentially, a nurse is always available as needed to provide comforting words over the phone or even make visits in the middle of the night.

The Labor of Death: What It Looks Like

Everyone dies in their own unique way. Often, the elderly have lost friends of the same age, parents, spouses, brothers, and sisters. Therefore, they understand death better than younger populations. Frequently, the dying know when they are getting close to death and are more accepting of this than their younger family members, who find end-of-life situations difficult. The stories in my book are about people between eighty and ninety years of age. By age alone, they have reached their life expectancy. Their stories take place in the hospice setting through a prolonged process of dying.

What happens when a person's body begins to let go? Just as we refer to a person's birth as the labor process, the dying process can also be laborious. Sometimes an event such as a stroke or heart attack can bring life to a sudden end. Sometimes the end comes slowly over a period of time.

When a person is dying, their blood pressure drops. The fast heart rate can no longer be sustained and drops, too. Breathing may run through cycles of fast and slow in the same minute. There may be longer and longer periods of no breathing (apnea) until breathing stops. Breaths can also become shallower with a "puffing" characteristic before the person passes. The lungs can fill up with fluid, and the person may not be able to manage the drainage coming from the mouth.

The person may or may not become unresponsive for a variable time before dying. But sometimes after a period of non-responsiveness, they become responsive again—sometimes for weeks. I like to think of this as a "trial" death. Perhaps the dying person feels the family isn't ready and so is in a "let's do this again" frame of mind (or heart). Regardless of how a person declines, the main goal of hospice is to provide a comfortable death and transition. Isn't this what we all want for our dying loved ones? To be of comfort, to offer something meaningful, no matter how small, before we leave each other? I remember asking Dad, while he was still able to eat, if there was anything we could get for him. We were hoping to get him to eat something after days of a poor appetite and eating only small bites of food. He wanted Pinwheels. Puzzled, I asked him what that was. He said it was a marshmallow cookie with a chocolate covering. Off to the store my sister and I went. As we numbly walked the isles, we discovered the sweet treasure. Finding those special cookies for our dad helped us feel better, knowing we were comforting him. In this small way, we offered him a bit of quality to his life too.

Signs of Progressive Decline

Many studies have shown that the less functional people become, the closer they are to death. The following list are ways to know that someone is declining.

- Gradual loss of appetite that shifts from eating less to eating only bites of food, with associated unintentional weight loss.
- The person's ability to feed themselves becomes difficult (due to spilling food, weakness, confusion, difficulty swallowing). The person moves from needing assistance to eat to ultimately needing to be completely fed. When the person is unable to swallow, they should no longer be fed or given pills to swallow by mouth. Mouth care can be given by moistening with minimal water such as with a swab.
- Progressive weakness that shifts from loss of the ability to stand, to falling, to sitting in a chair more, to losing the ability to hold oneself up in the chair, to inability to hold up one's head, to being bed bound and then unable to move oneself in bed.

- Bedsores may develop despite excellent nursing care and scheduled turning. Poor appetite is one cause for poor nutrition to the skin.
- Self-care declines from the ability to bathe, dress, groom, or use the toilet to requiring assistance, to eventually requiring someone to take on these functions for them.
- Multiple and/or increasing infections. The body may be unable to fight infection well with poor immune response. With each infection and treatment, it is likely that the person never completely returns to their normal baseline; instead, a new lower baseline is created after each treatment for infection.
- Mental status changes from confusion to drowsiness, to unconsciousness. As time gets closer to dying, the person may sleep for most of the twenty-four-hour day.

Chapter 3
SAYING GOODBYE

I believe our loved ones have the ability to hold the dying to this earth plane. In my experience, many people wait for the final goodbye from someone who is close to them before they will pass. This can be a spouse, a daughter or son, or a best friend from years ago. Sometimes the dying person will wait for a special someone to arrive from out of town before they pass. When a person is really hanging on—far beyond their physical decline—I ask the dying person and/or family and friends if there is a long-lost acquaintance or caregiver their loved one may want to see in order to say goodbye. I've seen many examples of this. Once, I learned that a man with dementia was hanging on long enough to see his ex-wife, whom he had not seen or communicated with in years. Realistically, not everyone can get in to visit on those final days, however most people are honored to be included as one who was special to the dying person in this lifetime.

Caregivers want and need to say goodbye to their patients too. Seeing caregivers come together to say goodbye to people they have cared for in a facility is heartwarming. Each staff member comes in at their choosing during their shift to say their unique goodbye. I once worked in an Alzheimer's facility where everyone was asked to say goodbyes in their own way. This included administrators, nurses, aids, the chef, and the social worker. Understandably, this was a tearful parting because in many cases, the staff had bonded with the person after years of caring for them.

Mark and Josefina: Comforting Words from a Spouse with Dementia

Mark and Josefina had been married for sixty years. On my weekly hospice visits to the home, I usually found them sitting together on the sofa. They were in their late eighties and would often be holding hands and even giving each other a gentle push to get off the sofa.

Josefina and Mark used their walkers to get around, walking slowly with a forward-leaning posture. Caregivers followed them to make sure they didn't fall. They ate meals together and slept together in their own room.

Josefina had dementia. She was forgetful and also hard of hearing. Even with her hearing aids turned up, we thought she couldn't hear us most of the time. As the events of Mark's decline became apparent to Josefina, she became increasingly angry by throwing things at caregivers and saying unkind words.

Mark's health continued to decline. He started having trouble swallowing and soon would not be able to swallow or eat at all. He had become increasingly weaker and eventually became bed-bound and unresponsive. After several days of Mark's unresponsiveness, Karen (an aide who cared for both of them) visited the home on her day off to say goodbye to Mark. Their three daughters stood by his bedside and had already said their goodbyes. His in-home caregivers had also said their goodbyes. At this point, Mark was going through long periods of not breathing with his eyes partially opened. He was very thin from weight loss, but he was still hanging on.

All the while, Josefina sat at Mark's side and observed these events. The day before he would pass, Josefina said, "Who is that person over there?" referring to her husband. We were not sure how much Josefina understood that her husband was soon to pass, or how she would react. She sat on another bed in the room, quietly observing the events of Mark's decline as it was happening. After a while, she stepped over to sit on Mark's bedside and patted him twice on each cheek. She then patted each eye, as if to close them. After that, she returned to her own seat, but within thirty seconds, she stepped over again to repeat the patting. Over the next few minutes, Mark's slow breathing became increasingly shallower. Just before his last breath, Josefina said, "Goodbye." She repeated "goodbye" as Mark took his final breath.

At last, we understood why Mark had hung on to life. He was waiting for his beloved wife to say goodbye.

Joe and Lisa: Daddy's Girl Says Goodbye

Joe was in the nursing home and in his final decline. He was not responding or communicating verbally with anyone. He moaned (a nonverbal sign of pain) at intervals. As a hospice nurse, my first challenge was to get a pain medication routine in place. Nonverbal signs of pain can be the stiffness with which one holds one's body, grimacing, moaning, yelling or crying. As hospice nurses, we are trained to recognize these signs in someone who might not be able to communicate pain verbally. There are several medical scales that rate a person's intensity of pain based on these observations.

At his bedside, I met Lisa, one of Joe's daughters. In conversation, I learned Joe had been in a slow decline for the last three months. He had always been an active athlete and had encouraged Lisa to participate in activities with him. She commented about long days on the golf course and then said, "You know, I was a daddy's girl!" She also admitted painfully that due to his suffering, she had prayed for him to pass.

Lisa had a special and loving relationship with her dad, but I wondered if she had actually been able to say goodbye to him. In our conversation, I said to her, "If this is true, then your dad may be holding on to make sure that you're okay. In his way, he's still trying to take care of you." Lisa didn't think she would be able to say goodbye at this point because her dad hadn't responded to anyone. I explained to her that he would understand and that it was time for her to say goodbye. I suggested that she might tell her dad, "I'll be okay without you and when you're ready, you can go to heaven," or wherever the family believed people go after death.

As I was leaving the hospital, I met Sandra, another of Joe's daughters. I shared the same information with her about saying goodbye. Sandra understood that her dad would hear her words even though he was not responding. She went up the elevator with the intention to say the final words she thought he needed to hear.

In my car, I recalled Lisa's words about praying for her dad to pass. I remembered praying for my dad to pass too and having a sense of guilt about that. I wanted him to move on to his new spirit life where he was no longer suffering.

Love takes on a new meaning in the dying experience. Rather than holding on to someone we love, we pray to let them go.

Joe passed away peacefully that evening, able to move on with the comforting words and expressed love from his daughters.

Chapter 4
HOW THE DYING CHOOSE WHEN THEY PASS

In the following stories, you will see how the dying choose their own time of passing and how my own intuition led me to follow through with patients even after they were no longer technically mine to care for. I will show how death was timed for me to be at the bedside to support a family. Intuition is a way of knowing that cannot be explained by a physical sense. I sometimes felt as though I was directed by spirit to be present with particular people. I also believe that intuition comes from being experienced, focused, open, and ready to receive.

Typically, these intensely poignant connections occurred with people with whom I had the closest relationships. These stories suggest that the dying put their family and special friends above themselves. They are willing to suffer a little longer to know they are leaving their family in good hands.

Victor and Rhonda: Choosing the Time of Death to Make It Easier on Your Spouse

Victor was on hospice at home. His wife, Rhonda, was always next to him in her chair when I visited. They sat in their respective living room chairs, and I'd pull up a stool between, facing them. I always called in advance to let them know I was on my way as I left the office for my twice weekly visits on Tuesdays and Thursdays at 10:00 a.m.

Victor was hard of hearing, so I really had to speak up. Often Rhonda would restate what I said. They had been married for fifty years, anticipated each other's thoughts, and finished each other's sentences.

Rhonda, who was also in declining health, was an oil landscape artist and had her own studio in the back of their home. I encouraged her to stay active with her art because it would help her cope through the decline of her husband. When I got to know them better, our conversations turned to art. I'd share my pictures of quilts, and Rhonda would show me her beautiful landscape paintings. We soon developed a friendship.

On the day before Victor passed, Rhonda called me directly (instead of through the office) to say that Victor needed a wheelchair because he could no longer walk and had been spending more time in bed. The next day, Rhonda called me directly again asking about the wheelchair. It was unusual for her to call me directly and twice within two days. I knew that I needed to get over there. It was the end of the workday, and I had made all my scheduled visits. I knew that something wasn't quite right.

I arrived to find Victor in bed, very confused. He looked to be very close to passing away. As I gave comfort medications, I told Rhonda, "Victor is very close to dying." She immediately left the room to call her daughter for what seemed like a long conversation. As Victor was about to take his last breath, I called out to her to come back into the room. She returned just in time to see Victor take his last breath.

I believe Victor wanted me there in order to comfort Rhonda at his time of passing. He had experienced such a slow decline in the background of many years of marriage, making it hard for Rhonda to know or believe that this day would be his last. But I also believe that I intuitively recognized something wasn't right; that sense of knowing is what made me decide to make the unplanned visit and arrive just in time to be present for both of them at this crucial time of Victor's passing.

Rhonda's health continued to decline, and she eventually made the move to a nursing home. Before leaving, she had an art sale and asked me to select a piece of her work to remember her by. Six months later, she too would pass. To this day, I think of her, especially when I see her painting that is a colorful landscape with a beautiful green tree, blue sky and clouds. I know that she's happy to have joined Victor in a setting similar to the painting she created.

Carlos and Lucia: A Nurse's Intuitive Knowing

Carlos and Lucia were a Spanish-speaking couple, but Lucia spoke enough English for us to be able to get through our hospice visit. I had taken care of Carlos in their son's home for about two years with weekly visits, so I had gotten to know them quite well. Sometimes, just prior to my arrival, Lucia would prepare warm tortillas for me. I was always so grateful because on most days, I didn't get a chance to eat lunch, and I appreciated the gift of sharing her culture with me.

Because Carlos and Lucia were devout Catholics, I'd spoken with the hospice chaplain to ask if he could make regular visits with them. He followed through by offering the sacrament and praying the rosary with them on a weekly basis. One day my visit coincided with the chaplain's visit, and I too got to pray the rosary. It was so heartening to pray the Catholic prayers that I'd learned from my childhood.

Lucia shared stories of being a migrant worker. I remember her stories about picking cotton and tomatoes and traveling each picking season to various farms. She shared her close connection with the other migrant workers. They shared meals and living spaces and took care of each other's children. After that, she owned her own Mexican restaurant, and that was where she'd met Carlos, a mariachi musician.

At this time, I had the opportunity to move to another hospice team in different area. However, I thought I could continue with the care of Carlos. After a while, the travel became difficult, and I had to pass his case to another nurse on the north team where he lived. About a year or so later, I was meeting with the entire hospice team in our weekly Monday morning review. This meeting was to discuss the on-call activity over the weekend. The hospice chaplain knew of my close relationship with Carlos and Lucia and commented that Carlos wasn't doing well. I thought, *I really ought to go over and see him.*

A few weeks later, on hearing the same comment again, I decided that would be the day. I contacted Lucia just after the morning meeting and asked if it would be okay to come by for a social visit later in the day. "Sure, Sure," she said.

I was on my way home later, after a long day, when I suddenly remembered I had promised Lucia a social visit.

I rushed home to check in before going over to their home about ten minutes away. I arrived about 6:00 p.m. Lucia opened the door and said, "I think he just passed." I went in and found the lifeless body of Carlos. After looking, listening, and feeling for signs of life, I determined Lucia was right. He had passed. I called the office to speak with the on-call nurse to inform her that I would proceed with the usual process that included calling the police (as per the city protocol), disposing of narcotics, and calling the funeral home. Lucia had already called the Catholic priest from her local church, who came in with perfect timing right behind me.

It was a miracle that I had shown up at the time of his passing after over a year away. If I hadn't, because it was after hours, an on-call nurse who didn't know the family would have made the death visit. I was grateful to have been there as a friend for Lucia. I believe that Carlos wanted me there to support Lucia and timed his death to my arrival. I also listened to my intuition and knew that I needed to be there.

Chapter 5
COMFORTING VISIONS OF SPIRITS

I believe we are spiritual beings in human form and existence. Through the process of dying, we are preparing to lose that human form and transition back to our spirit life. Often a person will tell me they are ready to go "home." When I hear this, I know that I must keep an open mind about the meaning of home. Home can mean their physical home, where they lived before coming to their current location. However, it can also mean the place they think of as the afterlife.

As death approaches, it isn't uncommon for one to have increasing visions of deceased loved ones. It's as though they are crossing a veil between this life and the next on a daily basis until they decide to stay on the other side.

I make sure to let families know about the visions

their dying loved one is having. Knowing that deceased loved ones are waiting for the person on the other side is comforting for the family. In addition, the family comprehends that death is approaching. Rather than experiencing only the overwhelming grief of loss, they also start to feel hope for the dying who will be with their beloved deceased family members in the next life.

Sarah: Visions of Deceased Family Members

I went to visit Sarah, who had been admitted to hospice at a nursing home. Sarah was talking, and oriented to her name. She said to me, "I was supposed to go home last Friday, but instead, I'm going home tomorrow." Sarah had dementia, so I wasn't sure what this meant.

When I checked with Sarah's daughter, Darlene, she was surprised because no medical person had discussed Sarah's discharge with her. Reportedly, Sarah had been seeing deceased loved ones, so I assumed that going home meant going to a heaven or afterlife.

Darlene wanted to know how many more days her mother had. I could give her only the signs that showed her mother was declining. One of those signs was seeing deceased relatives.

Sarah passed the next day. Sarah knew she was going home and could even tell us when.

Carol: Visions of Jesus

Carol was on hospice in an assisted-living facility. She was in her nineties, legally blind, and very hard of hearing. She'd started having falls and had gone to the hospital on at least two occasions to make sure she was okay. Each time, she went through the battery of tests to determine whether she had suffered a head injury. Although she had new bruises to her face, there was no internal bleeding.

Carol was hesitant to tell me about a vision she'd had. She wasn't sure I would judge her for what she was about to say. I encouraged her to tell me, saying that maybe I could help her. Cautiously, she opened up and described being seated on the bed when an unexpected light appeared in the room. From the light, a voice said, "they were getting ready for her in heaven." Carol, a Christian, believed this to be the voice of Jesus.

A couple weeks later, Carol reported a similar vision. This time, the voice said they were "almost ready for her." She contacted her daughter, Diane, who wasn't sure what to make of it and requested some simple lab tests to make sure that her mom was okay.

Another week passed before Carol would fall once again. This time, she had a head injury and passed away.

I believe the forewarning about the room being almost ready was just what Carol and Diane both needed to hear. They had received the reassurance that Carol would be going to heaven and meeting Jesus.

Chapter 6
OPENING TO SPIRIT TALK

Spirit talk is my understanding of knowing just the right words to say at a particular moment. For me, it's as though the words of spirit come through me. I think to myself, *Wow, did I just say that?* Sometimes the words are so profound that I feel they must be spirit directed or channeled.

In order to hear spirit talk, we must know how to listen deeply. Listening is a valuable communication skill. Being fully present and listening allows us to be more empathetic, but we can also hear the spirit behind the words. Presence is the ability to be fully in the current conversation with a clear mind, as opposed to thinking about the past or future. Chitchat in your head from a prior conversation or a personal issue can cloud incoming messages, making it hard to hear the heart of the incoming message.

One way to practice clearing your mind from chatter that clouds your ability to listen deeply is by listening to nature. On my daily walks, I listen for the sounds of birds. Anything else in my head is pushed out. Then I let the sounds of birds float through me, without thinking about them. The activity of walking itself calms my mind. Relaxing the body allows the mind to relax too. I have noticed after thirty minutes or so of walking, my mind is clearer. I also practice daily meditation. Through breathing exercises, I'm able to clear my mind and simply listen for spirit. Through this way of connecting with spirit, I'm better focused on the present throughout the day.

Richard: Channeling Words to a Daughter

Richard lived alone in a sparsely furnished home. His refrigerator was always empty except for a few condiments, although it appeared he was eating regularly because he always seemed to have fast food brought in by a friend. He spoke of being unable to pay his utility bills and unable to work due to his health. He lived in a run-down neighborhood that made me nervous to drive through or to park my car. There was construction going on in the house next door that scattered dust everywhere. One afternoon as I approached my car, I saw that not only was it covered in thick dust, but there were fingerprints on the windows as if someone had tried to get in.

Richard was forgetful when it came to taking his medications. When I suggested a pill box, he groaned about not having enough money for one. He said he couldn't remember to take his medications, anyway, because he didn't have a clock or watch.

Richard was divorced and had three children who didn't live with him. I had the opportunity to meet Richard's daughter, Daisy, at his home one day. She was sixteen years young with a tan complexion and long, smooth black hair. Daisy was wondering if she could do anything to help her dad. I asked her if she could remind him to take his medications and make sure he was getting something to eat. She promised to do this with a daily phone call.

Because Richard was a hospice patient, I was able to involve the whole team and especially a social worker, Lisa, who purchased a clock and pill box for Richard with her own money. She also stocked his refrigerator with a trip to the grocery store.

Richard continued to decline and later passed. I received a phone call from Daisy thanking me for everything I had done for her dad. This was a pleasant surprise of appreciation coming from this daughter I had spoken to only once. I asked her how she was doing, and she said something about taking a pause from school. She had a boyfriend, and it sounded like she was very much involved in the relationship. Oddly, she asked, "Is there anything I need to do?"

My immediate response, without thinking, was, "Stay in school." As soon as I said these words, I asked myself why I would say this to a near perfect stranger. I wondered if Richard was sending a message to his daughter through me.

Ruth: Intuitive Reception of the Perfect Words

Ruth's daughter had called the office requesting a visit for her mom, who was on hospice in a nursing home. It was December 24 around 4:00 p.m. I was the on-call person that day, so I headed out to see Ruth and her daughter, Tammy.

Tammy was concerned about her mom's swollen legs and how the drainage was coming through the dressings. Carefully, we unwrapped her legs and rewrapped them with the most absorbent dressings I could find.

Understandably nervous about her mom's decline, Tammy shared that recently Ruth had been nauseated and not eating well. However, on this day she had eaten more than in the past few days. I suggested at the time that maybe Ruth was happy to be surrounded by family.

There were a number of them waiting in the hallway for us to complete the dressing change.

Tammy said that her mom had been in a lot of pain, although it seemed managed on that day. She noted that her mom was weaker and less able to get to the bathroom on her own and had an episode of incontinence. I suggested that she might benefit from a bedside commode and a bed alarm. The bed alarm would sound as Ruth began getting up, alerting the staff to help her. Falling is an ongoing concern for all those on hospice, especially as they get weaker.

As I was leaving, Tammy followed me out to the hallway, and her family went back into Ruth's room. She asked if there was anything else she could do for her mom. My response was, "Enjoy her. Enjoy being with her. Enjoy her over this Christmas holiday. This likely will be your last Christmas with her." I felt these words just flow from me as if channeled, without thinking.

Tammy responded with a smile and said politely, "Okay." I was hoping that she could see beyond her mom's leg swelling, the drainage, the pain, the nausea, and the weakness. Rather, I hoped for her to see the love in her relationship with her mom. I encouraged her to leave the worry behind and just enjoy this present time. As it turned out, that was Ruth's last Christmas.

Self-Care for Caregivers

Strategies Learned over Many Years as a Professional Caregiver

It's important to practice self-care, especially when caring for the dying. Here are my suggestions learned over a career of taking care of others.

Sleep

The amount of sleep we need varies for each person. For quality sleep, go to bed and wake up at the same time every day. Limit soda, tea, coffee, and chocolate because as we get older, our bodies hold onto these longer. Alcohol can cut the amount of time we spend dreaming, which is essential for quality sleep, so keep that limited too.

Eat Healthy

Don't skip meals. Eat slowly and mindfully, putting your fork down between bites. Stop eating before you are full to allow your satiety hormones to catch up. Eat routine meals and fill half of your plate with vegetables and fruits.

Drink Water

Provided there are no health limitations, carry a refillable water bottle to drink throughout the day. The body needs water to function but also to help us to think and feel better.

Meditate

For its calming effect, I encourage you to develop a spiritual meditation practice.

Exercise

Take time each day to get your body moving to your level of ability. Consider stretching as an activity.

Nature

Enjoy the multisensory experience of being in nature. See the blue sky and green trees, hear the birds, and smell the roses. If it's safe to do so, walk barefoot to feel the grass and grounding earth.

Gratitude

Practice gratitude for all that is, including family, friends, pets, and nature.

Chapter 7
ANGELS AS GUIDES

I often hear a family member say they fear a loved one might be alone when they die. In my experience, I know we are not alone because I have felt the presence of what I call angels around me. As a nurse, I believe that sometimes the angels want me present with the dying person and at other times, not. This can be a tricky time to manage symptoms and yet give the dying person space by stepping out. In families where I have established a strong bond, I've learned that my presence is often needed for the loved one to take that final breath.

Sometimes people prefer to die surrounded by family, or certain family members. However, it is also common for loved ones to pass at just the time a family member gets up to go to the bathroom. Regardless of whether our earthly family is physically present, we will still be guided through death by what I believe to be angels.

Katharina: Angels Arrive at the Time of Death

I was assigned to the care of Katharina, who lived in her own home. The hospice goal, in addition to maintaining her comfort, was for her to die at home.

As usual, visits included many questions about whether she was eating, sleeping, or having pain. She suffered from intermittent periods of confusion for which multiple causes were considered. We had determined that she had developed an infection for which antibiotics were prescribed. However, after two days of antibiotics, she stopped swallowing, became unresponsive, and couldn't take more medicine.

Katharina lived close to the office and was rapidly declining, so I decided to visit every day. On this beautiful sunny day without a cloud in the sky, I arrived to see that she was struggling to breathe and actively dying. I explained to the family that it wouldn't be long before she would pass. It was the end of the day, so I decided to stay on past my scheduled time to help everyone through Katharina's passing. Because of the time I'd already spent with the family, I thought I could be more of a comforting presence than an on-call hospice nurse who didn't know them.

As I stood at the bedside, I heard what I considered to be an "angel voice" that wanted me to step out of the room. Actually, the voice was demanding that I do so. I stepped out of the room and spoke with other family members who were in the living room area. The sky suddenly became a dark grayish black, and outside a heavy downpour hit the ground hard. As I stood there, I could feel my feet tingling, and I experienced a chill with goose bumps. A breeze passed through me, although there was no open window or explainable reason for it. I felt the presence of spirits surrounding me. At this moment, I would learn, Katharina took her last breath.

I tended to the post-death arrangements but most of all comforted the family the best I could. One son, Jakob, said to me, "We couldn't have done this without you."

"It was my honor and pleasure to work with you, your family and your mom," I replied.

As I was leaving, I could see that it was a beautiful, bright sunny day without a cloud in the blue sky. It was as if Katharina had moved the clouds on her way to the afterlife. This seemed to be her final way of saying thank-you.

Ethel: Intuiting Angels at the Bedside

Ethel had resided in a nursing home for many years. For the last five years, she'd been on hospice. With a diagnosis of dementia, she was unable to communicate, dress, or bathe herself. She was incontinent, bedridden, and unable to even move in bed. Her bottom was scarred from healed bedsores. She had a feeding tube on a pump that continuously delivered the amount of liquid calories she needed to maintain her weight. Her medicines were given to her through the feeding tube by the facility nurse, Joan, who had become quite attached to Ethel. Joan had worked at the facility for as long as Ethel had been a resident. She had watched Ethel decline over the last four years and wasn't ready to accept that someday soon would be her last.

I had assumed Ethel's care from another hospice nurse who had moved on to a different territory. It was hard for me to understand Ethel's prolonged life considering her condition.

In a phone conversation with her daughter, Jane, I asked if she had seen her mother lately. She said it had been a year or so because she lived in another state. My next question was whether or not she was aware of her mom's current condition. I detailed her dependent health status and asked if this was the way she remembered her.

Jane then said, "My mom never would have wanted to live this way."

Ethel developed a lung infection, and crushed antibiotics were added to the stomach tube for a week or so. At first, she seemed to be improving. Jane agreed that keeping her comfortable through hospice would be best. However, a few days later, when I visited her again, Ethel was struggling to breathe. To make it easier for her, comfort medicine was given. The liquid food being pumped into her stomach from the feeding tube was not being absorbed but rather going up to her mouth and down into her lungs. Ethel's body was shutting down, and she was actively dying. The feeding pump was turned off.

I stood at the bedside and could see she would stop breathing for forty-five seconds to a minute. However, she then would surprisingly take the next breath. I could feel a coolness in the room and a tingling sensation in my feet and legs. It was as though there was an electrical charge in the air. I had goosebumps. I could sense the angels standing on each side of me and across the bed. As I overlooked Ethel from the bedside, it felt as though there were four spirits there.

After watching her breathe like this for twenty minutes or so, I realized that maybe the angels were waiting for me to get out of the way. I thought I should step out of the room for a few minutes. It was an odd thought to be waiting for angels to "do their thing." When I came back in, Ethel had passed.

I called Jane to let her know her mom had passed. After all these years, Ethel passed under my care within our short amount of time together. I am grateful to have been chosen as the one to help her in her final days.

John: A Procession of Angels in Human Form

In this next story, I believe not only that angels were awaiting John's final passing but also that it's possible the people present in physical body were angels.

John had dementia but had become suddenly unresponsive after a hard fall that affected his brain. He was well liked by residents and the staff at the assisted living facility. I was in his room discussing his case with the bedside nurse when I noticed a tall person with white hair walk by the single small window in his room. The window pretty much framed a person's head. The white-haired man was elderly and looked straight ahead, giving us a profile view from where we were seated. He walked at a brisk pace with a bit of a forward posture. The area outside the window was within a grassy courtyard.

A few minutes later, I noticed an entire line of people walking past the window. I wondered if maybe this was an exercise class but thought it was odd, because elderly patients usually don't exercise in a grassy courtyard, where they could stumble on uneven ground or rocks. In general, their gaits were brisk and independent with no walkers or assistants. This too was unusual.

All of the walkers were looking forward, and not one turned to look into the window. In general, the stream of elderly continued to walk by the window for thirty minutes or so and included about twenty-five people. Many of them walked by several times.

After the visit with John, I asked one of the nurses if there was any activity for the residents out in the courtyard that day. The answer was a firm no. There would rarely be a walking activity in the courtyard, particularly because there weren't too many independent walkers in the building. On this day, there was no activity planned because the activities director was out.

Chapter 8
HEALING GRIEF WITH LOVE

At death, I believe that we take love with us. Our love is nonmaterial and crosses to the next life. I believe those who have passed before us still look out after us with loving intentions from their new home. I believe that in our loving relationships, our love doesn't end at death.

When family members visit, it's upsetting for them to see their loved one struggling in any way. In the following story, you'll see how addressing the comfort needs of a mom, Christina, allowed me to have a meaningful conversation with her son. Through our conversation, I was able to help him process his relationship through fond memories of his mom. He was grieving for the mom who was healthy, the way he'd known her. He knew she would soon pass. As always, it's important to address comfort needs, but especially as the final days of life approach. Rather than remembering how his mom appeared to suffer, he was able to process his own grief and remember their happy days in a lifetime together.

Christina and David: Healing through Photos and Deep Listening

Christina was an elderly lady on hospice in a nursing home. She was in the last stage of dementia, was very confused, and had been suffering with a blocked bowel. She wasn't able to eat because food could not pass through the blockage of stool in her bowel. The family had been given the option of surgery to unblock her, however they decided against it. Surgery would prolong Christina's life considering that she would soon pass from advanced dementia.

When I got to her room, she was restless, moving all over her bed. She had managed to pull her clothes off and strip the bedding. I suspected that Christina may have been anxious from being wet and possibly in pain.

I had planned a meeting with her son, David, and expected him in his mom's room in about thirty minutes. I wanted to get her calmed down and cleaned up before his arrival and requested a facility aid to help me. By the time David arrived, his mom looked peaceful. I let him know she'd been restless and that she could be suffering in pain. With her condition, it was likely she would need scheduled medication, because she would not be able to ask for anything or even know herself that she was in pain. Because she was unable to take anything by mouth, we could give her medicine under her tongue that would absorb and dissolve to relax her.

The room was quiet as David and I sat down and started to talk about his mom's decline. He opened up about her life as a mother and a nurse, and her fondness for roses. David shared that he had recently lost his father. It was clear that he was grieving his dad's loss, the loss of the mother he once knew, and the soon-to-be final loss of his mom. He'd brought a scrapbook of old photos with him that we looked at together. I could feel that David really needed someone to talk to, so I decided to be there for him by moving my other, less pressing visits to later in the day.

Christina passed just a few days later. I was glad to have arrived earlier on that prior visit so David could focus on the fond memories of his mom, rather than her uncomfortable appearance. Perhaps his dad was there in spirit to help David through me. Dedicating extra time through listening to David was my gift of love to his family.

David wrote a thank-you note that I still have. "I want to express a heartfelt appreciation and gratitude for the tender loving care provided by Lynda. She was an angel for my mom and me, as I was having a meltdown. She pulled me through. I will always remember her."

Rosa: A Comfortable Death Experience Heals the Family

In the next story about Rosa, you will see how I was challenged to provide Rosa and her family a peaceful death. An uncomfortable death means the family's last memories will most likely be about the death experience rather than the memories of a lifetime of love and relationship. The family would be caught up only in the memory of the death itself and unable to progress through their profound grief.

Rosa was a retired nurse who lived in her home with her husband, Miguel. On my first visit, I got a good sense of family dynamics. The family was still grieving from the loss of Susan (daughter and sister) to cancer several months earlier. It had been a very sad experience and involved watching their loved one suffer with a "tremendous amount of pain." The family was caught up in the experience of Susan's death rather than who she had been as a person. They could hardly grasp that Rosa too might also be preparing to pass.

Miguel was in chronic back pain with a limited ability to walk. He seemed confused at times, possibly related to his own pain medication. His daughters were very concerned about their dad's ability to physically care for Rosa. They arranged intermittent home healthcare visits to check on Miguel while I arranged increased frequency of hospice visits through the week for Rosa.

Over the following weeks, Rosa would remain comfortable through the increasing doses of pain medication. Monitoring her pain through medication adjustments was one of the challenges in her care due to the increasing severity of pain that she experienced over time. The family often made references to where Rosa was in the disease process relative to Susan's decline. They often shared their sadness of Susan's loss.

Due to Rosa's end of life decline and need for symptom control, rotating shifts of hospice nurses were assigned to her care. These nurses were continually at her bedside through their shifts. I was grateful for the ongoing twenty-four-hour support that was offered to this family.

I received a call from a hospice nurse saying that Rosa had become unresponsive. I made an immediate visit and found Miguel in the yard watering his tomatoes. I thought it odd that he wasn't inside with his wife in anticipation of the visit. As I stood there silently beside him, he asked, "How long do you think it will be? A week, a month, or year?" He seemed profoundly sad and was looking down, not making eye contact. Behind his question, I could hear his denial that Rosa's passing could be soon.

"I'm not sure, but I'll go in to see her. Please come in so we can discuss her condition," I said.

A few minutes later, Miguel came back into the home and into the bedroom. I explained that Rosa had low blood pressure, and her heartbeat was a little fast. She had just started having breathing changes, and a dose of morphine had been given. While her symptoms were under control, she remained unresponsive. I shared with Miguel that passing could be within the next few hours. He immediately stepped out of the room to call his daughter. I heard him say, "You'd better come on over because she's getting ready to pass."

This family was experiencing layers of grief and up until now had been in denial about the possibility of Rosa's death. Now they would all come together at Rosa's bedside to witness her final passing. I suspected that Rosa would wait until her entire family would be present before she would choose to pass. This would include one daughter who lived an hour away.

The family requested to see their local community church chaplain, and that was immediately arranged. Miguel, his two daughters, and the chaplain were present at Rosa's final passing. Perhaps Susan was there in spirit to assure this would be a peaceful transition and therefore provide the family much needed healing. The chaplain would later write a note of gratitude to hospice. "Rosa's death was one of the most spiritual deaths I have ever witnessed."

I felt a sense of peace in knowing that I had prepared Rosa and helped her family through their grief. I was glad the family members were all present at the bedside to experience Rosa's peaceful passing. I had provided the comfort and support this family needed to not only grieve Rosa's death but also to move past the death of Susan.

Andres and Wanda: Changing the Grief Perspective

In this next story about Andres, you will see how he and his wife, Wanda, struggle in their day-to-day relationship through Andres's decline. In their struggle with sadness, they miss the big picture of love in their relationship.

I had come to see Andres for our weekly hospice visit. Wanda was always present. They had a large home with grand windows that overlooked a beautiful, landscaped golf course. They had been active golfers, but with time Andres decreased his activity due to lower energy and, eventually, chest pain. When Andres realized he could no longer muster the energy to play a day of golf, he was happy to walk the shorter distance to the club restaurant, splitting up the walk with a meal before returning home. When he wasn't sure that he could make it at least one way, Wanda started following him with a wheelchair in the car. She said it eventually was too challenging for her to push him up the hill or to hold him back while going down the hill. At this time, however, Fred could barely walk a few steps across the room without experiencing chest pain.

I could see that Andres's loss of ability to walk and the thought of his eventual passing was affecting Wanda emotionally. In their retirement, they had done most things together and in support of each other. However, I could see that she felt helpless watching him decline. She was grieving not only his eventual passing but also their joyful and loving relationship as she knew it.

Andres was feeling down as he watched people on the golf course, doing what he wished he could do. He was grieving for the loss of his active life. I said to him, "You should focus on what you can do, not what you can't do."

I asked him to consider trying virtual golf on the computer. He had no idea that this game even existed. As Wanda listened in, I said, "Maybe the two of you could compete against each other." Wanda smiled, and her complexion seemed to change from exhausted to radiant. I sensed these words were just what she wanted to hear.

I returned a week later for another visit. Andres was excited to tell me how he had discovered virtual golf. He said, "It's so much fun!" By engaging in a new activity, at a level that Andres was able to manage, Andres and Wanda could work through their feelings of grieving, but more important, they enjoyed their love for each other in those final days.

Pablo and Judy: Pablo Heals Judy and His Caregivers

Pablo had passed away in the locked dementia unit of an assisted living facility. I happened to be walking through the facility hallway on my way to the same unit. To my surprise, I saw Judy, his wife, sitting there in a hallway chair. Judy was also a resident of the facility.

It is my usual practice to contact the family of the deceased to say that I am sorry for their loss and wrap up our working relationship. This is especially so when a person passes after hours, and I'm not there to help them through it. However, I had not made that contact with Judy for various reasons, so I was glad to see her.

As we talked in the hallway, she said, "It takes a special person to do what you do." Judy seemed to be accepting of her husband's passing and commented that he was blind and very hard of hearing. However, in heaven she believed he could see and hear, and she was very happy for him.

Judy had been sitting in the hallway that I usually walk

down to see my patients, but it was not the hallway where she resided. She had been waiting for her daughter, who was coincidentally late. If her daughter had been on time (thirty minutes earlier), I wouldn't have run into Judy.

Judy said that she could never return to the dementia unit where Pablo had passed because it brought back memories of his death. I suggested that she visit the area because it would bring healing to her and to the caregivers in the area. The caregivers were grieving as well because Pablo had been a long-term resident. I wondered if Pablo had arranged the circumstances for our meeting. He may have been there with his new sense of sight and hearing to help us all grieve and heal.

Chapter 9
SHARING LOVE THROUGH NUTRITION

As the body shuts down, so too does the need to eat. The body uses its remaining resources for circulating blood to vital organs such as the heart, lungs, and kidneys. The person isn't hungry. It is incorrect to say they are starving to death. Starving is what happens to healthy people who want and need food and can't get it.

In the usual progression through decline, the person will still be able to feed themselves but will eat less and less. With increasing weakness and/or confusion, someone will have to feed them. This means buying, preparing the food, setting them up at the dining table, and spooning food into their mouth. Then comes more difficulty swallowing followed by total loss of the ability to swallow. This is when the person should no longer be fed at all. Why?

Normally when food goes into the mouth, it moves down to the stomach. However, if the person cannot swallow the food, it can go into the lung tube instead of the tube to the stomach. This is called aspiration, meaning the food going into the lungs sets up a kind of pneumonia.

In order to feed a person food, the person must be awake. If they aren't awake, they don't know they're supposed to swallow. This sets up another way to have trouble breathing and can ultimately cause death.

Educating family and friends not to feed their loved one is one of hardest things I've had to teach in hospice. To most people, feeding means getting stronger and getting well. To the contrary, at end of life, feeding can cause suffering.

From a spiritual perspective, I often see the struggle of family trying to feed the dying. By understanding that food is not a priority, the loving relationship is restored. The struggle suddenly leans toward understanding and love instead of a desperate need to try to feed a person whose basic needs have changed.

Betty and Cindy: Feeding an Unconscious Mom

Betty was an elderly woman in a nursing home. She had been unresponsive since the previous night. When I stopped by for my hospice visit, her mouth was gapping open and she was experiencing the beginning signs of trouble breathing.

Betty's daughter, Cindy, was at her bedside. The nursing staff had just brought in a food tray. I think Cindy assumed that it would be okay to feed her mom because the tray had been brought in. The nursing staff had not yet received the order for no food by mouth. I advised Cindy against feeding her mom and explained the reasons for this. Because Betty was unresponsive, she would not know to swallow any food put in her mouth.

As I was explaining this to Cindy, she seemed confused. She asked, "Can I just try to give her a little bit?" Clearly she didn't hear my words and was intent on feeding her mom anyway.

I had to catch a phone call and stepped out of the room. When I returned, Cindy had put what looked to be three large spoonsful of mashed potatoes into her mom's dry open mouth. I did my best to gently scoop them out.

There was no use explaining why Betty didn't need food. I realized that Cindy couldn't hear me through her fear and anxiety about her mom's dying. I decided it would be best to start a conversation about her relationship with her mom. The real issue was Cindy's fear of loss and love. Her intent was to nourish her mom the way her mom had once fed her.

Lois and Anne: The Struggle with a Mom Who Refuses to Eat

Lois lived in the home of her daughter, Anne. Lois had dementia. At first, she could stand with lots of assistance to transfer to her wheelchair. With time, she couldn't stand at all and became bed bound. She couldn't speak and was developing additional behaviors that often come with dementia.

As Lois continued to decline, she ate less and less. Then one day, in a seemingly intentional act, she clamped her mouth shut. Anne tried her best to get her mom to open her mouth. This often involved coaxing her mom with favorite foods or placing the spoon to her lips, hoping to initiate jaw opening. Just when we thought Lois wouldn't eat again, she would start taking bites.

Clearly, Anne was distressed by this. I said, "She will eat if she will. You can only do the best that you can do." I wanted Anne to know that feeding her mom was no longer a priority. There was no need to force or coerce her mom to do anything. I hoped she would understand that her loving relationship with her mom should take precedence over anything else at this point.

Eventually Lois clamped her mouth shut and kept it shut. In the end, not only did she refuse to open her mouth, but also she couldn't swallow. The conversation became, "Don't feed her."

Anne was able to understand and accept the place her mother was in at this point in the dying process, and she could be a loving presence to her mom in those final days. Lois soon became unresponsive and passed. I was glad Anne could remember her mom as she was in her lifetime of their loving relationship instead of the memory of fighting with her mom in order to get her to eat.

June and Beth: Hydration Isn't a Priority

In the next story about June, her daughter, Beth, is concerned about dehydration (lack of fluid in the body). Most of the time, to get intravenous (IV) fluids into the vein by tubes, a hospital stay is required. Going to the hospital is often difficult for the debilitated because it is a change from their routine and usual environment. The change in environment and routine can cause hallucinations, uncooperative behaviors, anxiety, and extreme confusion. It's also difficult for the person to endure the transportation to and from the hospital with its bumpy rides and transfers from home to vehicle to hospital considering the person's weakness, weight loss, boney appearance, and pain.

Offering IV fluids can cause one to have to go to the bathroom more often. If a person is unable to hold their urine, then urinating in the bed can cause a bedsore, especially if the individual is mostly bed bound. Also, because many elderly suffer from a weak heart, offering extra fluids can cause their heart condition to worsen, making it hard to breathe and accelerating death.

However, at this stage dehydration can actually be a good thing and can induce a kind of euphoria. At end of life, the goal is not hydration. Being tethered to a plastic tube line running into the arm vein can be painful, especially when trying to maintain the ingoing fluid arm site. For infection control purposes, the IV insertion site is changed routinely every three days. However, a person who is confused may pull out the tube several times a day. The tube can also be a source of falls because it can easily become entangled in someone with a weak gait.

June had just returned from the hospital. This was her third time there for dehydration in the last few months. Each time, she had been given IV fluids and then had the tubes removed at discharge. She was sent back home to continue eating food and drink by mouth for her hydration. June was on hospice and living at home with her daughter, Beth, who took care of her.

As a result of minimal eating and drinking, June was getting weaker by the day and required assistance with feeding, walking, bathing, and dressing. Beth was frustrated and said, "She just won't eat. We might have to go to the hospital again!" She was still concerned about dehydration.

I explained to Beth that June would accept food and drink as she wanted to and could. It was okay to offer her mother food, but if she didn't want it, it shouldn't be forced on her. I explained to her how dehydration is a good thing at end of life.

Once Beth realized she didn't need to worry about how much her mom ate, dehydration, or returning to the hospital again, she was able to focus on her mom and their relationship. I was glad to have helped Beth understand that hydration and many of the things that are healthy and necessary for a well person were no longer important to her mom, a person in the dying process. This enabled Beth to enjoy the last few weeks with her mom. June eventually stopped eating altogether and passed peacefully at home weeks later.

Chapter 10
HOW FORGIVENESS HEALS THE DYING AND THE LIVING

Holding a grudge against another is like carrying a heavy burden. To forgive allows one to be set free of an oppressive weight. In the case of a dying person, asking for or receiving forgiveness may be just what is needed for that person to pass.

Family members who ask for forgiveness from their dying relative can start to process and even mend their relationship with the dying person. By releasing their burden, they are better able to move through the grieving process. Giving or receiving forgiveness can be a healing experience for both parties.

Mabel: Forgiveness Heals an Unresponsive Mom and Her Daughters

It was the weekend, and I was called out to see Mabel, who was unresponsive and bed bound. She was at the end of her life. Her daughters, Kelly and Katie, were teary-eyed at her bedside. There was tension in the air apparently related to the rocky relationship between the daughters and their mom. I could clearly see there was need for emotional healing.

I pulled each daughter out of the room individually, but neither would share any detail about their relationship, although each daughter made it very clear that something had happened in the past that was absolutely unforgivable. Still, they were grieving and at her bedside, so I felt there might be room for them to reconcile.

I asked each daughter to talk with their mom individually. At first, they were resistant. They had this "Mom's beyond hope now" attitude. I let them know that Mabel could still hear them even though she wasn't responding. I encouraged them to speak from their heart with their own history of relationship and feelings. I asked them to forgive their mom for whatever it was that seemed unforgivable. Then I asked them to ask their mom to forgive them for how they responded or what they may have done that brought disharmony into their relationship.

They were not willing to share their story with me, but Kelly commented that there was a lot to be forgiven for. I wasn't sure whether there were several incidents or one grand incident. I asked her to go ahead and say as much as she was willing to say. The goal was not just to say these words but to help heal the daughters by unburdening them through forgiving their mother, using their own words.

Mabel passed four hours later. Hopefully, the daughters were finally able to reconcile at least a part of their sadness and find healing. I believe Mabel was able to let go through the words her daughters were finally able to share.

Doris: Daughters Forgive Each Other to Help Mom Pass

Doris, who was on hospice in the hospital, was unresponsive. When I first met her, she was surrounded by her daughters, Shelly and Susan, and their families. The room was crowded but oddly quiet. I felt that Doris may have been the glue that held them all together.

Over the coming days, Doris seemed to hang on. She remained unresponsive with a very concerned and anxious family surrounding her. The nursing staff reported that they didn't understand why she was still hanging on to life.

I asked the family if everyone had said goodbye. They had already learned that saying goodbye was important and had done so in their own ways. When I asked if there was anyone else who might have been important to Doris, they shook their heads no.

In a later conversation with Shelly, she said, "My mom always favored my sister, Susan, who had a lot of health problems when we were growing up. I felt kind of left out." She went on to explain her sister's health issues, and as she did, she became visibly upset and started crying.

As she cried, I said, "Your mom needs to know that her family is together and will support each other when she passes." I suggested that she have a heartfelt conversation with her sister.

The next day, Shelly said that she had reconciled with Susan. Susan had not been aware of this reason for sadness and distance in her sister. I asked Shelly and Susan to let their mom know they had talked it out and that everything was okay. Finally, Mabel understood that her family was truly together. She had been waiting for them to make amends before passing that very evening. In so doing, the daughters were able to fully support each other in their grieving over mom's passing.

Chapter 11
COMFORT THROUGH RELIGION, MUSIC, MEDICINE, AND INTUITION

As I hope I've shown, a person must be comfortable to peacefully pass away. When a person passes peacefully, the family can be more present in their grief. The family can remember the positive moments of the relationship and move through their grief more easily rather than live with the memory of an uncomfortable death.

We've spoken about physical comfort for the dying person, but comfort can also come from a spiritual perspective. When I first meet a hospice patient, I always consider their commitment to faith and spirituality. If they were active in their church, temple or mosque, I make it a point to include the hospice nondenominational chaplain in their care. For those who are Catholic, I arrange for a priest to visit who will offer anointing of the sick.

Music from a person's chosen faith can sometimes be comforting at the bedside, particularly for people who have a deep connection and long-term memories of singing or chanting in their church, temple, or place of worship. I've witnessed families and friends bring in favorite CDs, play YouTube videos of kirtan or a loved chorale, or in some instances sing together around the bedside. Sometimes family and friends aren't sure what is appropriate to offer at their dying loved one's bedside. Hospice encourages sharing anything that will bring comfort. This kind of loving attention comforts the dying and can be part of the tender and positive memories long after the person has passed.

Jack: Finding Comfort through the Music of His Church

Jack was a Christian man and former minister who felt fulfilled by the teachings of Jesus. He was hopeful for his reunion with Jesus in heaven. Barbara, Jack's wife, had told me about the church group who met at their house on Sundays. Their son, Andrew, was also a minister and in search of property for a church, but in the meantime, his small congregation had been meeting at his parents' house. I thought what a blessing this must have been for Jack, who really needed the support of his son and their friends, especially as he was nearing death. The group was right where they needed to be not only to support Jack but also for their own spiritual growth.

On several of my visits, I brought my mandolin and played gospel tunes for Jack. His favorite song was "In the Garden." On some visits, I'd coordinate with the hospice chaplain, who would sing from the hymnal as I played. Jack was so appreciative of our musical visits and found comfort through them. Two days before he passed, I went for a social visit (not required by work) to play the mandolin for him. I could see that he was actively declining because he was more breathless than ever when talking, to the point of intermittent confusion.

Later, as I returned home, I had a significant, heart-opening realization. I had always wanted to be a better mandolin player and had struggled to learn because I was self-taught. I suddenly realized that if I had learned the mandolin only to comfort this man in his last days, then that was as good as I would ever need to be.

Annie: The Power of Music to Reach Dementia Patients

My family volunteered to do an hour musical concert for the residents of a dementia facility. The patients all had moderate to advanced dementia, meaning they couldn't carry on a meaningful conversation or bathe or dress themselves. Several could not walk or talk at all.

I played mandolin, my husband played guitar, my daughter played the flute, and my son the bass clarinet. We weren't coordinated enough to play the same songs together but instead each played individual songs of our choice, and we completed our concert within an hour.

As we played, some of the residents sang along with beautiful voices. It was interesting to observe that they couldn't remember basic hygiene or even how to tie their shoes, yet they could sing these songs by heart once they heard the music from their childhood days of singing in church.

As our time was completed, Annie stood up in front of us, facing the crowd. She had been a teacher and confidently addressed us now. "So, what brings you here today?" Annie had been one of the people singing along wholeheartedly with the hymnals, yet once the music stopped, she couldn't remember anything about that past hour.

Leticia: Offering Comfort without Medicine

As the labor of death approaches, it is ideal to bring pain under control. By doing so, the dying person is at peace and better able to make the transition. In hospice, we have a "comfort kit" with medications to care for fever, pain, anxiety, agitation, nausea, and constipation. The kit is ordered at anticipation of nearing death, so it will be available for bedside use. Most of the time, all comfort needs can be met in the hospice-guided home setting, except for intractable pain. In this case, a pain medication is delivered through an IV to more closely control the discomfort. Unfortunately, constipation is a distressing symptom often brought about by pain medication. For this reason, anytime pain medicine is ordered, the potential for constipation must be addressed.

We had just completed our weekly hospice Monday morning meeting. I was in the office, finishing up paperwork from a busy weekend. My manager, Raul, texted me asking for my help on an admission that needed to be done, although hardly any information was available on the case. I was handed a phone number and an address. Raul let me know there had been screaming in the background of the phone conversation, but he had no further information about what was happening.

This sounded like an urgent admission with a person

in extreme discomfort. I said a prayer as I got into my car, asking for help in getting safely to this woman and for the guidance to help her. I didn't have the pain medication that she would need because Raul was in the process of ordering it through the doctor. I wasn't sure how I could help her, but I trusted that by praying for divine help, I would be guided to figure out a way to ease her pain and distress.

Once I put her address in my phone, I realized it would take about thirty minutes or so to get there. When I was about ten minutes down the road, Raul called me and asked for an expected time of arrival. I wasn't really sure considering traffic and the fact that I had never been to this address. He let me know he'd received another call with the woman still screaming in the background. Raul was doing his best to contact the attending doctor for a script of pain medication and was frustrated because the response was slow. "If only the doctor could hear this lady screaming, he might be more vigilant."

As I was driving, I received yet another call from Raul and one from Rita, the daughter of the screaming woman, asking how much longer I would be. When I arrived, Rita was standing in the driveway. Her first question was, "Do you have the pain medicine?" I apologized and said that I didn't, but arrangements were being made through the doctor at the office. I asked her if I could see her mom, and maybe I could do something to help while we waited for the medication to arrive. Rita directed me up the tall flight of stairs that ended at the back door to the home. Her mom was at the top of the stairs to the left.

As I raced up the stairs, I could hear Leticia yelling. A bit out of breath, I took a left into her room. She stopped yelling momentarily and gave me a look of, "Who are you?" As I introduced myself, she began screaming again.

I moved closer to her bedside, leaned over to within inches of her face, and looked directly into her eyes. I asked her in a firm and commanding voice, "Where. Is. Your. Pain?" I surprised myself by approaching her this way, because normally I am a quiet and reserved person. I felt as though I had been directed by spirit to address her in this way that was so out of character for me.

Leticia responded, pointing toward her waist as she lay on her back in the bed. I asked, "Are you constipated?" Rita had told me that she wasn't sure, but her mom might be. I asked, "Is it okay to check her for constipation? I'll look at her rectum, if it's okay." Understand that I had been in the room for less than a minute, with someone I had never met before. At that nod, Rita and I assisted Leticia to her side, and I was able to extract the stool. She continued to scream, but when enough stool was removed, she became calm.

Rita said, "Wow, you really did come in the back door,

didn't you?" It was a literal statement. I was surprised that she could make a joke after such a distressing event. I called the office and spoke to Raul.

"Well, she was constipated, and with a little help she's okay."

"Thank God!" he said.

To myself, I thought, *Yes, gratitude for my answered prayers that allowed me to use my intuition and be guided to help this woman get relief from her excruciating pain.*

Nonverbal Signs of Pain: Ways to Determine if a Person May Be in Pain

- Facial Expression: grimacing, frowning, quivering chin, clenched jaw, or teeth grinding
- Body Activity: squirming, tension, aggression
- Staying in Bed: sometimes people will stay in bed because it hurts them to move
- Pacing or Wandering: Some people will move around a lot because being still makes them feel their pain more
- "Voicing" without Words: moaning, whimpering, crying, or screaming

Chapter 12
PRAYER TO HELP THE DYING

Prayer, which I believe is communication with the Divine, is integral to how I practice hospice work. I have always been a prayerful person and have certainly prayed for my patients and families. I most often pray that I will be able to help people get what they need. Sometimes the answer I receive is an answer to their prayers. There is a certain comfort in knowing that through prayer, we may be helping a dying person, especially when we aren't sure on our own how to help. I find that prayer not only helps the person but also helps me find my own healing.

Gratitude is an expression of love within which spirit works. I find that prayers of gratitude spark a positive energy that helps me connect deeper with spirit. I will often begin my prayers and meditation with gratitude for the love of my family, including my dogs, friends, my guardian angels, the sounds of birds, the beautiful trees, health, healthy food, home, and my career as a nurse. The more things I find to be grateful for, the more I notice in my abundant life.

Virginia: Praying for Healing at the Bedside

I had come to the office early on this particular day and had already done my paperwork in anticipation of our weekly meeting. I was thinking I would read up on a clinical procedure I wasn't familiar with. I was a little bit of a perfectionist, so it was very unusual that I wasn't anxious about getting everything done up to the minute before our meeting.

I noted that several managers were hovering around one desk, clearly distressed in both their words and manner. I had heard a former patient's name mentioned and asked if there was some way I could help. Brenda, the manager for the central team, responded, "I don't know if you can help, because this daughter is clearly driving us all to our own end!"

"Well, do you mind if I go out and see her? Maybe there's something I can do because I know her and the family?" I said.

"If you think you can, go ahead!" Brenda replied.

Virginia was in a nursing home at this point. Previously

her care had been given by the hospice team in the home of Ginger, her daughter. In most past visits, Ginger was tearful and often hadn't gotten much sleep the night before. She was generally exhausted. So when I saw that Virginia had moved to a nursing home, I was glad because her poor daughter needed a break. I would learn later that Ginger had been visiting her mom in the nursing facility daily for several hours at a time. She was very particular about her mom's care and would make signs to post on the wall reminding the nurses what they needed to do.

When I arrived at the nursing home, I checked in with Virginia's facility nurse. He said that Virginia seemed to be hanging on, and he didn't know why. She had been in end decline for over two weeks and was receiving routinely scheduled comfort medications. Ginger, who would typically be there at this time, had just left and said she wouldn't be back until the next day. I thought this sounded unusual but was grateful to have some time alone with Virginia.

As soon as I entered the room, I could see that Virginia was unresponsive. The room was very quiet, and this seemed a good opportunity for me to pray over her. I pulled up a chair and held her hand. I silently prayed for the angels to take her on to heaven. I prayed for her to find an end to her journey and move onward to a place where she would no longer suffer. I also prayed for Ginger's comfort and eventual acceptance of her mom's passing.

I grounded myself in prayer by standing up and planting my feet firmly on the floor. As I held my hand just over her head, I asked for Spirit to come through me for Virginia's healing. I don't know what gave me the idea to do this, but I accepted that maybe it was a divine thought and an answer to my prayer. Through healing, I hoped for the angels to lead her on toward a peaceful death. I sat with her a bit longer, holding her hand again and gave her permission to go. In a compelling voice, I said, "Now, Virginia, it's time to go to heaven. You don't need to stay here any longer. Your daughter will be okay without you. She will see you again someday on the other side."

I spent about thirty minutes at the bedside praying for her. This left me just fifteen minutes to get back to the office for a meeting. As I entered the meeting room, Brenda asked, "What happened?" She and another manager gave me a dazed look, as if something incomprehensible had happened.

"What do you mean?" I asked.

"Well, Virginia just passed."

Aileen: "Your Prayers Are Answered!"

I was assigned to Aileen, who was living in the home of her daughter, Karen. Aileen required twenty-four-hour care and had a diagnosis of dementia. Karen worked long days at a restaurant, so during the day, Aileen was watched by a paid caregiver. At night, Karen took care of her mom. Karen had reached a point of exhaustion, and at the recommendation of a friend, had chosen to go with hospice.

Aileen had been admitted to hospice over the weekend, so I was meeting her for first time. As, I came into the home, Karen was clearly distressed and shared her feelings of overwhelming fatigue. Aileen was very restless at night, so Karen slept in an adjacent room with one eye open and her ears perked because she feared that Aileen would suffer a fall.

Karen started talking faster and faster, and as the words came, so did her tears. Then she said, "I have been praying for a miracle to help me through this."

I paused and then said, "Your prayers are answered. I'm here to help." I explained that not only was I there, but the entire hospice team would be seeing her soon and offering support.

What I didn't tell Karen was that the night before, I had prayed that my patients scheduled for the next day would get just what they needed. I had prayed that if there was a miracle through me, I would be honored and humbled.

I really do believe that I was assigned to Aileen's case so that I could meet Karen and be part of the answer to her prayers. And through divine intervention, Karen also answered mine.

Manuel: Praying for a Way to Communicate

Our manager sent a message out to the nurses on our team. It read something like this: "Can anyone speak Spanish? Even if you can speak only broken Spanish, please let me know."

After some thought, I responded with a phone call. I explained that I spoke broken Spanish and had taught children basic Spanish words and phrases at the elementary level. I had taught them topics such as colors, numbers, days of the week, months of the year, and body parts. The children's favorite subject was pet and animal names. They loved to hear the story of how I had pet ducks and chickens as a child. I used to walk around with chickens on my shoulders as we made chicken sounds together and bobbled our heads forward. I would also get on the ground and quack with my ducks.

Manuel and Maria were Spanish-speaking only. I felt my first home visit was sort of a flop and my Spanish-speaking skills were all over the place. Incorrect verb tenses and the words "no me entiendo" (I don't understand) still rang in my head.

As I sat in the car preparing for my next visit, I prayed,

Please help me communicate with this family and help me understand what they need. Just after I knocked on the door, Maria asked me to come in. She said, "*Entre,*" with a smile. The home health aide was in the other room assisting Manuel with his bath. I could hear the bilingual hospice aid speaking to Manuel in Spanish.

Maria and I would have a chance to talk as they finished up. I could already feel myself sweating and wondering if I could somehow talk as though I had been speaking Spanish all my life. Then Maria proceeded to tell me (in Spanish) about her and her husband's adventure to the park the previous weekend. She said they went to the park by the church and fed the ducks (*los patitos*). I couldn't believe it—I understood everything she said.

I also learned at that visit that Manuel's son (who lived in the home) was bilingual and could speak English well. I knew that our relationship was going to work. In more ways than one, my prayer had been answered.

Praying for the Dying through Poetry

Often we get confused about what to pray about when we are losing someone we love. After all, the person is dying and on hospice. Our natural instinct is to pray for our loved one to get well and recover, but at the end of life, disease and a failing body require us to see things differently. Loving a dying person is about wanting the best for them, and that means letting them go. A more helpful prayer may be about saying goodbye, asking for comfort, love, peace, hope, forgiveness, support, strength or direction. Depending on your belief system or religious orientation, prayer can be about spiritual healing or finding the next life.

Through my own experience with death, I offer you a prayer of mine that was inspired by sitting with dying patients and their families. It isn't meant to be recited verbatim but rather offered as words to your heart to help you find and say your own prayers.

I WILL PRAY FOR YOU

I will pray for you
To get comfortably through today.
I will pray that you will find comfort in
forgiving those who hurt you,
And that you will forgive yourself
for those you have hurt.
I will pray for you to be grateful,
Even to those who have been hateful.
I will pray for you to get through this
By finding support of those that you miss.
I will pray for you to know
Whom to turn to and where to go.
I will pray for you to find new hope
As you discover ways to cope.
I will pray for you to receive grace
As you work through grief's pace.
I will pray for you to have enough strength
As you endure each new day at its length.
I will pray for you to accept help,
Especially as things change and develop.
I will pray for you to have the support
of family and friends,
From those who care for you, and not necessarily kin.

I will pray for you to feel calm
As you find answers to your questions
through prayer or psalm.
I will pray for you to let go and to say goodbye
As time moves forward, and your
loved one is soon to die.
I will pray for your soul to dance
As you find the next life at first glance.
I will pray to spirit around us and above
That you will always feel the presence of love.

Final Thoughts

I hope these true stories that come to you from the loving and intuitive perspective of a hospice nurse comfort you through your fears of dying. My wish is that the tools I've presented—intuition, prayer, empathic listening, forgiveness, letting the angels in, accepting Spirit visions at the bedside, accessing the Divine—will be helpful as you tend to your loved ones in the process of passing. May you see the love inherent in your grief and in those who are grieving around you. May you trust and know that the love in our relationships continues after death.

Blessings on your journey.
Lynda

About the Author

Lynda Noll has been a licensed nurse for nearly forty years, caring for hundreds of patients and their families through the end of life. Angels at the Bedside is her first book. For more about Lynda and her writing, visit www.lyndanoll.com.

www.ingramcontent.com/pod-product-compliance
Ingram Content Group UK Ltd.
Pitfield, Milton Keynes, MK11 3LW, UK
UKHW041432311225
9831UKWH00035B/298